SELF-HELP TECH SUPPORT

Computer Hardware/Software/Wireless Network Repair,
Customization and Optimization

MONICA OBOAGWINA

AuthorHouse™
1663 Liberty Drive
Bloomington, IN 47403
www.authorhouse.com
Phone: 1-800-839-8640

First published by AuthorHouse 9/23/2009

ISBN: 978-1-4490-2381-2 (sc)

Library of Congress Control Number: 2009909434

Printed in the United States of America
Bloomington, Indiana

This book is printed on acid-free paper.

authorHOUSE®

Dedication

Dedicated to those that do not have a computer; and people who provide the opportunity for the poor to have access to modern information technology.

Acknowledgements

Special thanks to my colleagues, Joe Wilker and Zang Vang for their professional advice, and Ekawat Suwantaroj for helping with the graphics. I am grateful to the editors, Dr. Ruth Poochigian, OP and John Schmitz. Thanks to Dr. Mary Ellen Gevelinger, OP, an author herself for the suggestions about publishing. Thanks to my religious Congregation, Dominican Sisters of Sinsinawa for financial and moral support. To all others who contributed to the birthing of this book, know that I am grateful. Above all, thanks be to God for everything.

Contents

Abbreviations

AOL	-	American Online
AMD	-	Advanced Micro Devices (chip)
ATA	-	Advanced Technology Attachment
BIOS	-	Basic Input and Output System
C	-	Copy as in Ctrl C
©	-	Copyright symbol
CD	-	Compact Disc
CD-R	-	Compact Disc Read only
CD-RW	-	Compact Disc Rewritable
CMOS	-	Complementary Metal Oxide Semiconductor
CPU	-	Central Processing Unit
Ctrl	-	Control key
DCIM	-	Digital Camera Images
Desktop	-	Tower or mini-Tower computer. It also refers to computer screen, e.g. my desktop is blank.
DIMM	-	Dual in-line Memory Module
DNS	-	Domain Name Service
DOS	-	Disk Operating System
DPI	-	Dots per inch as in clarity of a picture
DSL	-	Digital Subscriber Line
DVD	-	Digital Versatile Disc
DVD-R	-	Digital Versatile Disc Read only
DVD-RW	-	Digital Versatile Disc Rewritable
DVI	-	Digital Video Interface
ESD	-	Electrostatic Discharge
Fn	-	Function key

FTP	-	File Transfer Protocol
GB	-	Gigabytes (Billion Bytes)
HTTP	-	Hyper Text Transfer Protocol
HTTPS	-	Hyper Text Transfer Protocol Secured
IDE	-	Integrated Drive Electronics (a cable that connects the hard drive to the motherboard)
IE	-	Internet Explorer
I/O	-	Input and Output
IP	-	Internet Protocol
ISP	-	Internet Service Provider
LAN	-	Local Area Network
LCD	-	Liquid Crystal Display
LED	-	Light Emitting Diodes
MAC	-	Media Access Code; it is also an abbreviation for Macintosh computer
MB	-	Megabytes (Million Bytes)
NTFS	-	New Technology File System
OS	-	Operating System
PC	-	Personal Computer
PCI	-	Peripheral Component Interconnect
PDF	-	Portable File Format
PPI	-	Pixels Per Inch as in image resolution
®	-	Registered Trade Mark
RAM	-	Random Access Memory
SATA	-	Serial Advanced Technology Attachment. (It's a newer cable technology that connects the Hard Drive to the motherboard)
SCSI	-	Small Computer Systems Interface
SDRAM	-	Synchronous Dynamic Random Access Memory
SSID	-	Service Set Identifier
TB	-	Terabytes (Trillion Bytes)
TM	-	Trade Mark
URL	-	Uniform Resource Locator
USB	-	Universal Serial Bus controllers
V	-	Paste as in Ctrl V
VGA	-	Video Graphics Array
WEP	-	Wired Equivalent Privacy
WWW	-	World Wide Web
X	-	Cut as in Ctrl X
XP	-	Express as in Windows XP trade mark

Introduction

Many times helpdesks have limited staff to handle the high volume of support calls. This can result in higher hold times or delays in answering your technical questions. The answer may be as simple as restarting the computer. Having the knowledge of simple technical tools will help you avoid long hold times or a long conversation. Not only do you save yourself from frustration from long tech support calls but you also get your computer up and running quicker.

I experienced this long waiting on the phone with my home laptop. After the initial automated response, I waited about 30 minutes before a tech came online. I explained what the problem was and the troubleshooting I did up to that point. I was expecting a grandiose response. The tech on the phone simply told me to restart the computer in safe mode. I asked, "Is that all?" He said, "Yep." I did and it worked. And I was a tech!

I really feel for users to get their computer, email or internet access working, especially when working on a project and the system is not cooperating.

I was impressed as a tech by Jim. He called because the computer wasn't logging him off when he clicked start, log off and ok. I started instructing him to hold down the power button for few minutes to force a shutdown so that the next time he logs in, he should be able to log off normally and Jim patiently said, "I already did that. It didn't work". I said, "Ok, unplug the power cable from the computer and he repeated, "I did that too", stressing, "I don't want to have to unplug the power cable each time I want to log off." I agreed. I commended Jim for his tech skill in trying to fix the problem before contacting me. I told him I'll come over to run anti-virus software; that it's probably a bug that locks up the log off button. (Munz 2008).

Jim did the basic troubleshooting before calling for tech help. Wouldn't you feel excited to find an easier way to figure out a problem by yourself? Even if you don't find a solution and you need to contact tech support, at least you can explain what technical troubleshooting you tried so far. The tech will know you are no novice and you'll be proud of yourself when you speak technical language!

When you maintain your system frequently you acquire technical skills that need no special study, no school fees, and no testing. Some technical skills you will find in this book have been learned from experience and not in computer text books. Experience is the best teacher. Given that computers are here to stay, now as common a household item as a TV, you need a few basic skills and wisdom and brevity to handle urgent situations and periodic maintenance. You will find this I-can-do-it-myself book a handy tool for home and small businesses. It is an instructional technology.

- It answers some frequently asked questions.
- It helps you customize features of your choice, such as what you like your screen display to look like, the font size, or your own text written screen saver.

You may find some of the contents too elementary in this book. However, you would be amazed at how many computer users don't know about fixing simple computer problems or customization.

This book can also be used to teach computer basics to kids and adults in vocational learning centers.

- Computers are called by different names, including: node, system, machine, PC and box. I used some of these names here.
- Notebook is another name for a laptop, which is a physically smaller and portable computer. I didn't distinguish it when I say computer.
- You may have a tower, a mini-tower, a notebook or mini-laptop (called net book or atom). In this book they are each referred to as a computer or a system.

The software platform referred to in this book is Windows Vista® and Windows XP® operating systems. While their graphical interfaces are different including some feature locations, the formats are similar. For instance, Help and Support is the same method and in the same location. Fixing a computer problem is similar in both operating systems. Some word processor examples are from Microsoft Office 2007 ®, specifically, Microsoft Word 2007 ®.

Mac ® users with the Apple ™ operating system can also find this book useful for basic computer maintenance and repair. Users will find that there are some variations, even within the same operating system, depending upon the versions being used. In a nutshell, this book can be useful regardless of what computer hardware or software is being used.

1. Computer freezes

1. Turn off the computer.

    • If you cannot turn off your PC normally by going to **Start> Shutdown**, hold down the power button for 10 seconds to force a shutdown.

    • If that fails, then unplug the computer. (Remove the battery if it's a laptop).

2. Wait 10 seconds or more for the hard drive cylinder to stop spinning and cool down.

3. Turn on the computer.

Note: Powering the system off and on is also referred to as power recycling the computer. If this quick solution doesn't resolve the freezing, do the following A through C:

A.   *Delete cookies and temporary Internet files*

Windows Vista and Windows XP:

1. Right-click on the **Internet Explorer** (IE).

2. Scroll to **Internet Properties** and click it.

3. Under **Browsing History** click on **Delete** to bring up choices for deletion.

4. Delete **Temporary Internet** files; the system will ask if you are sure, click yes; delete **Cookies**. Close window. Click Ok.

5. You don't have to restart if you are in the middle of something. It's okay not to restart, even if the computer prompts you to do so.

Note: If you delete history you will lose all the website addresses you've visited in the address box. Take a moment to ask yourself if you really want to delete history.

Internet Explorer is the blue e icon on your desktop. If it does not appear on your desktop, go to Start menu, in the lower right corner on your screen, and find it at the top of the menu.

If your Start menu is configured in the classic mode, IE should be on your desktop or on the bottom left corner near Start. If it's not, click on Start, then Programs, look for Internet Explorer and right-click on it. (See Chapter 32 for the difference between classic start menu and start menu, and how to customize them).

If you are already online using internet explorer, click on **Tools**. Scroll down to select **Internet Properties**.

1. Under **Browsing History** click on **Delete** to bring up choices for deletion.

2. Delete **Temporary Internet** files; the system will ask if you are sure, click yes; delete Cookies. Close window. Click Ok.

B.   *Delete temporary files:*

Anytime you install software or download files online, it leaves files in a temporary folder; empty this folder regularly. You do not need these files.

1. Double-click the icon for **My Computer**.

2. Double-click **C:** local drive (also called Hard Disk Drive).

3. Look for **WINDOWS** folder and double-click it.

4. Find **Temp** folder and double-click to open it.

5. By-pass the yellow folders and highlight the first sub-folder.

6. Hold down the **Ctrl** (control) key on the keyboard and click the rest of the sub-folders to highlight all.

7. Delete the selected items by clicking the X on the left hand menu of the screen; you can use the keyboard delete key.

Sometimes a file may not delete, and will hold up the deletion. If this happens, hold down the Ctrl key and click on the stubborn file to de-highlight it. Let go of the mouse and click on the Delete icon to delete the rest.

A faster route to go in selecting folders for deletion:

- Instead of by-passing the yellow folders,
- Highlight the first one,

- Hold down the **Ctrl** key and

- Click on the last yellow folder.

- Release the shift key.

- Go to the top menu and

- Click **Edit**, scroll down and

- Select **Invert Selection**. This feature will deselect the yellow folders and highlight all the sub-folders.

- Go near the top left corner under File and Folder Tasks, click the X that says delete the selected items. You can use the delete key on the keyboard.

C.   *Run anti-virus software*

There are different types of software to rid junk information and cookies that are unintentionally collected and saved on your hard disk every time you visit the internet. Free anti-spam software, such as the following, can be downloaded online:

http://www.malwarebytes.org

http://www.ccleaner.com (same company as http://www.crapcleaner.com)

http://www.adaware.com or http://www.lavasoft.com

http://www.spyware.com

http://search-destroy-download.com/

Here is what can happen to your computer while online even though the description refers to Sybot software specifically:

"Spyware is a relatively new kind of threat that common anti-virus applications do not yet cover. If you see new toolbars in your Internet Explorer that you didn't intentionally install, if your browser crashes, or if your browser start page has changed without your knowing, you most probably have spyware. But even if you don't see anything, you may be infected, because more and more spyware is emerging that is silently tracking your surfing behavior to create a marketing profile of you, that will be sold to advertisement companies...... Spybot-S&D can also clean usage tracks, an interesting function if you share your computer with other users and don't want them to see what you worked on." (Spybot para.1, 3).

2. Computer runs slowly

- Do Steps A to C in chapter 1 above.
- Delete files, documents and pictures you don't need to free up space on the hard disk. Or store them on a flash drive, CD or any other external media storage.
- Add more memory to the computer.
- Rebuild the computer (See Chapter 12 on how to rebuild a computer).
- Take it to a PC repair store
- Buy a new computer as the last resort if problem persists.

3. Defrag computer periodically for maintenance

Defrag when you won't use the computer for at least an hour. Defrag takes one or two hours, depending on how scattered the cylinder is in the hard drive. Defrag collates all the fragmented files on the cylinder and closes up the gaps:

1. Click on **Start** in Windows Vista (or Windows XP).

2. Click on **All Programs**.

3. Go to **Accessories**.

4. Scroll down to click on **Systems Tools**.

5. Select **Disk Defragmenter**.

6. Click on **Defragment now**.

7. When finished, click **Ok** and then **Close**. Restart the system.

Defrag in Windows Vista

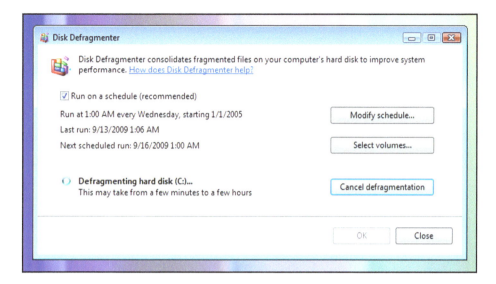

Microsoft product screen shot of Windows Vista ® reprinted with permission from Microsoft Corporation

4. Install free computer updates from software/hardware manufacturers for its increased lifespan.

Tune up your computer with the newest patches, updates, fixes and latest versions by downloading free from the manufactures' websites. You cannot afford to buy a new system each time a product is released in the market. As technology changes, vendors develop updates to meet up with the latest requirement; to rid viruses; to introduce a better component; to enhance computer durability.

Microsoft Corporation ® for instance, makes available critical updates enhancement, to get rid of spam; for backward compatibility with new released software versions as in Microsoft Office 2007 working with Microsoft Office 2003. Hardware updates are provided periodically by the makers of Chips, Bios, Network cards, Audio cards. You can download drivers for your computer components, printers, scanners, cameras, PDAs (Portable Data Assistants) from manufacturers' websites.

Know the serial number or product name of your computer or the version of your software to get information quickly from the vendor's website. Know the logo (the maker's brand name). A laptop serial number is located on the bottom in a barcode format. Towers and mini-tower computers' serial numbers are at the back or in front. Dell ™ computers serial numbers are called service tags.

Here is a list of some major hardware/software vendors' websites:

- www.dell.com/support
- www.hp.com/support
- www.lenovo.com (The website will ask you to select your country).
- www.ibm.com/support
- www.gateway.com/support
- www.apple.com   http://www.apple.com/downloads/macosx/apple/
- http://www.apple.com/softwareupdate/
- http:/global.acer.com (The website will ask you to select your continent).
- www.compaq.com (click on get support). (HP ™ bought out Compaq). You can go directly to the redirected website at http://h18000.www1. hp.com/cpq_support.html (Note the underscore between cpq and support.html).
- www.adobe.com/downloads

Besides going directly to the Adobe ™ website, it is possible to update an Adobe application when it's open; click on Help, scroll to Check for Updates. Make sure the computer is online for the update to download. Examples of Adobe applications are Photoshop, InDesign, Acrobat Professional; Acrobat Reader, Illustrator and Premier.

- www.microsoft.com/downloads www.office.microsoft.com

There are different versions of Microsoft Windows; look for the Windows updates icon in its menu. Find it under All Programs, click on it to go to Microsoft website if you are online. Another route to get to Windows updates is: when online, using Internet Explorer, go to Tools on the menu browser, scroll down and click Windows Updates.

An example of free updates is Microsoft Windows Update:

Microsoft ® sends out updates, typically every Tuesday, which fixes bugs and security issues in Microsoft software. These fixes improve the quality, security and stability of Windows and Microsoft Office software. It is recommended to do Windows update at least once a week. Un-patched computers can lead to viruses, spyware, software and windows operating system crashing.

There are two methods of updating - Express and Custom. Express downloads and installs all critical updates, whereas custom allows you to choose which updates to install.

Express Update:

1. Open **Internet Explorer.**

2. Type in the address http://update.microsoft.com and press **Enter.**

3. Click on **Express.** (This may take a few minutes to compile a list of updates).

4. Click on **Install Updates.**

5. Restart the computer after the update is completed.

Custom Update:

1. Open **Internet Explorer.**

2. Type in the address http://update.microsoft.com and press **Enter.**

3. Click on **Custom.** (This may take a few minutes to compile a list of updates).

4. Click on **Optional Updates** and select your choice.

5. Restart the computer after the update is completed. (Windows Update para 2).

5. A quick way to shutdown and restart a computer

Besides the common method to shut down and restart, the following works with fewer clicks:

1. Press **Alt Ctrl Del** on the keyboard.

2. Click **Shutdown** and **Ok.** To restart, click the arrow down, select Restart, Ok.

To cancel, click **Cancel** and the computer will go back to the previous screen.

6. Three ways to do a force shutdown

When a computer seems to just hang there instead of shutting down, it is either trying to close a program that is not responding, or the system is just too slow. If it seems to take forever, try the following:

Option A: Press and hold the physical power button for few seconds and the system will automatically shutdown. Give it two minutes if you want to restart. This allows the hard disk cylinder to finish spinning and cooling down.

Option B: Unplug the power cable from the computer.

(Pulling the plug will not work on a laptop. The battery continues to power the system even if you unplug the power adapter, unless you take the battery out as well. Do option A above to force a shutdown on a notebook).

Option C: Switch off the power from the main source, i.e. unplug the power cable from the wall or the surge protector.

Note: if you do a force shutdown, the computer will not restart normally. After a power on self-post, Windows operating system will alert you to the previous abnormal shutdown and will ask you to choose options for Windows to boot to, for example, **Last Know Good Configuration**. Windows automatically saves files, though some files maybe corrupted if forcing a shutdown frequently. In essence, do not use these steps if you don't have to. Microsoft Windows operating system recommends normal shutdown and restart.

7. If the Computer does not boot to Windows operating system

1. If the computer is on, press the CD/DVD drive button.

2. Insert the original Windows CD that came with your computer into the CD/DVD drive.

3. Press and hold the power button for few seconds to shut down the system.

4. Wait for few seconds, and then turn on the computer.

5. As soon as the computer logo comes up, press **F12** on the keyboard for few seconds. (The logo is the name of the computer maker, e.g. Dell, HP, Compaq, and Lenovo). This stage is called POST (Power-On-Self Test) where the computer first tests all the components within it. F12 commands the system to open to boot menu.

6. In the boot menu, press the arrow down key on the keyboard to scroll to **CD/DVD drive** option. (**Note:** the mouse will not function during the process).

7. Press **Enter**, Windows runs until it comes up with options to install or repair.

8. Select **R**, press enter; wait few seconds for more Windows instructions and command prompt **C:** When you see **1. C:\Windows>**

9. Type **1** and press enter.

If it asks for administrator's password, type it in if you know it. It may be necessary to call and ask tech support for the password. Usually vendors build computers meant for home use without administrator's password.

10. At **C:\Windows>** type **chkdsk** and press enter. You will see
    C:\WINDOWS>chkdsk

(Chkdsk stands for check disk). Windows starts checking and ends with the same command prompt. If there are no errors, it reports that the volume is in good condition. If you want to run a thorough check disk, type chkdsk / and press Enter. Note that there is a space before the /p. This is what you will see,
C:\Windows>chkdsk /p

When Windows finishes checking, you will see a detailed report.

11. Remove the CD and restart the computer. (**Note:** some computer makers have built-in repair instructions. If you are not sure, call the tech support.)

8. Test computer hard drive/components periodically for proactive diagnosis

1. Shutdown the system and wait for a few seconds

2. Press the power button to turn on the computer

3. As soon as the logo comes up, press **F12** on the keyboard for some seconds

4. Use the arrow down key to navigate to **Hard Disk Diagnosis**. Press enter.

This program tests the hard drive and other components such as the Floppy Disk drive and the DVD drive. When completed take out the CD and restart. The result will show the components that passed the test and those that failed. If the hard disk fails, the program stops and asks if you want to continue the test.

9. How to backup your system

Backup makes a copy of your hard disk files so you use it to restore your local hard drive if it is ever necessary. Even when the hard drive is damaged beyond repair, it can be replaced with a new one and the copy can restore your system files, pictures and documents to their original state.

1. Go to **Start, All Programs, Accessories, System Tools** and **Backup**. The backup wizard window opens to welcome you

2. Read the options available to you and click **Next**

3. Select **Backup files and settings**.

4. Click **Next**.

5. Choose the items to backup and click **Next**

6. You can choose the place to save the backup. If you do not want to save to the default Drive A (Floppy drive), click **Browse**; click **Cancel** when the system asks you to insert the disk into drive A. It will open another window for more storage choices. Flash drive and CD are some external choices.

    If you want CD, insert it into the CD/DVD drive bay; if flash, plug the USB flash drive into the USB port.

7. Click on the drop-down menu to select your choice of storage location

8. Double-click your preference or highlight it and click **Save**. In the **file name**, it defaults to Backup. You can change the file name. In **Save as type**, be sure it's **Backup files (*.bkf)** extension.

9. Follow the onscreen instructions to complete the backup.

10. How to save files and folders on an external disk drive in case the hard drive crashes

Besides the Microsoft Windows operating systems backup utility that enables you to backup your hard drive, flash drives and mini external hard drives are other ways to save your files on. They are getting cheaper. It is highly recommended to save valuable files and documents on these removable disks. Some people use CDs or floppy disks. The removable drive can be stored in a safe place other than your desk. It becomes very handy if your system hard drive ever grinds to a halt. Your local hard drive may not be repairable if it goes bad. At least your important files and documents will be safe somewhere. A portable drive fits easily into your pocket or purse.

The illustration is from Windows Vista Home Premium.

1. Turn on your computer and let it boot to Windows Vista.

2. Plug in the USB flash drive into the USB port. The operating system will automatically recognize and installs the driver after which it will inform you that your new hardware is ready to use.

3. Open the document you want to save. Go to **File**, click it. (If you are using Microsoft Word 2007, click on the Microsoft Word logo which is the 4 squared colors in a round circle on the upper left corner pictured below.)

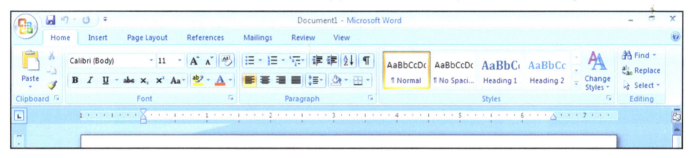

Microsoft product screen shot of Word 2007 ® reprinted with permission from Microsoft Corporation

4. On the drop-down menu, scroll to **Save As**.

5. Once you make your choice, Word will open another window where you choose where to save your document; this is when you select your removable drive by clicking on the arrow down. The drive will show as Removable Drive F or G as the case may be. It depends on the fixed drives you have on your computer. For instance, a laptop may have Floppy Drive A, the local hard disk will be Drive C and the CD/DVD drive will be Drive D. In this case your flash drive will be Drive E

6. Highlight the removable drive and click **Save**. You can double-click it too and the document will be saved. You can rename the document.

Note: Do not simply unplug the USB flash drive to remove the device until the system indicates that it is safe to remove the device. Do not be deceived by the message, "safely remove the device" that appears by merely pointing the cursor to the icon.

Follow this procedure:

- Double-click the USB drive icon on the taskbar near the time. (Green and Grey color). Double-click on the highlighted **Mass Storage Device** to expand it.

- Select the drive you want to remove; it will highlight automatically.

- Click **Stop**. A message will indicate it is safe to remove the hardware. Unplug the device, and click **Close**.

See the examples in screenshots:

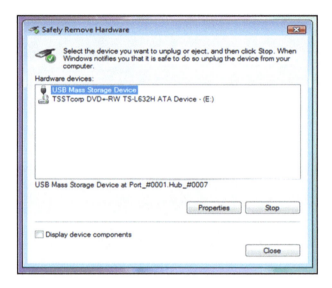

Microsoft product screen shot of Windows Vista ® reprinted with permission from Microsoft Corporation

Microsoft product screen shot of Windows Vista ® reprinted with permission from Microsoft Corporation

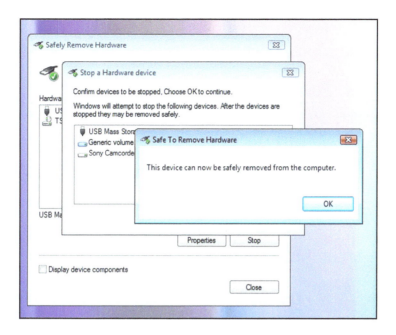

Microsoft product screen shot of Windows Vista ® reprinted with permission from Microsoft Corporation

11. Using System Restore to restore your computer to the state it was in before the problem started

A problem can occur after any change is made to your computer, such as software/ hardware installation, an update, downloading a program or driver. This may result when the new installation is not compatible with your system's hardware components or the version of your operating system.

Some of the symptoms include:

- The operating system may not run well
- The operation system gets stalled as it tries to boot up and may continue to restart automatically instead of booting to login screen.
- You may see blue screen.
- You may get error messages when opening a program
- You may experience "not responding" in some applications
- The system may restart itself in the middle of your work
- "Not found" error message may appear on the screen when you want to connect to the internet.

System restore can solve these problems. Your saved files, documents, favorites, emails, pictures, applications and programs are intact when you run system restore. You do not lose anything up to the point the trouble started.

Two ways to get to System Restore

- One way is within the operating system, e.g. when you are on your desktop screen.

- Another method is shutting down your computer and restarting it while holding down **Ctrl** key and **F10**. Some vendors set F11 command for this function. The cold boot format is necessary when your computer doesn't boot to Windows.

Within Windows Vista for instance,

1. Go to **Start**, click on **All Programs**, **Accessories**, **System Tools** and **System Restore**

2. Check **Restore Computer to an Earlier Point** or check **Create a Checkpoint**. Click **Next**.

3. The next dialogue page provides more options that are self-explanatory. So is the whole process. System restore pretty much has clarity with easy- to-follow instructions.

You can cancel anytime or go back to the previous page except during the restoration itself. You will be instructed to not turn off the computer while system restore is running.

12. Rebuilding your computer when necessary

Some vendors, i.e. computer manufacturers, have integrated re-installation files in the system setup. Acer computers with Windows Vista for instance, have this feature. Acer customers can purchase the E-Recovery CD if the reinstallation files are badly corrupted. New Dell computers come with a reinstallation CD. You can use System Restore as instructed in chapter 11.

Know what is available to you before rebuilding the computer using the following instructions:

A. Windows Vista is our first installation tutorial. It is self-explanatory, so I will not go into too many details.

1. Insert the CD into the CD-ROM drive, and the setup will take it to the setup screen if you are within the previous installation. Press Enter to boot from CD or DVD. If you are starting from a cold boot (turning off your computer and turning it on), tap on **F12** three times once the vendor's logo screen appears.

Select the **Onboard or USB CD-ROM** drive. And Windows installation will pick up from there.

A dialogue screen appears for you to customize the language, time, currency and keyboard input. You do not have to change any of the default settings if they meet your specific needs. You will see **Collecting Information number 1** with a light green color filling the bar at the bottom of the screen.

2. Click **Next**.

The next screen is a menu of options: **Install now. What to know about Windows Vista; Repair. Read Licenses terms.**

3. Click on **Install Now** and check **I accept the License terms**. Click **Next**.

Another customization page lets you select upgrade or custom install. It warns you that the custom install is an advanced and clean install that does not keep your files, settings and programs. It adds that if you do not know which to choose, click on **Help me to decide**.

When I was installing mine, the upgrade image was grayed out and disabled. Setup advised me to start installation from Windows if to upgrade.

4. **I chose Custom Install** and clicked Next.

The screen opens to the drive and its capacity to install on. You may click on each menu to learn more. Format if to erase all contents of the hard disk. Delete icon will erase the partition and data. Load Drive icon requires a media (CD or flash drive) that contains the hardware drivers. As you read each menu, click the blue arrow on top left corner to go back to the main menu page.

Note: If you do not make a choice and just click next, Windows alerts you to the fact that files, settings and data will be saved as Windows.old. You can access them, but not from the previous Windows install.

5. I chose **Format** and clicked **Ok**. The setup takes few seconds to change to the next page. Click **Next**.

Windows installation starts and you will see the incremental progress in percentage and a light green color spreading inside the bar on the bottom of the page named **number 2 install windows**. Installation continues to put a checkmark on each menu it has completed. It tells you your system will restart few times during this process. So don't panic when the monitor goes blank.

When the installation is finished, Windows will restart. This message appears briefly: **Press any key to install from CD...** (It asks because the CD is still in the drive). Ignore it unless you did Fdisk (See Chapter 57). The system will boot to Windows Vista. Type your name, a password and choose a picture for your name. Password is typed twice. The operating system lets you choose a password hint in case you forgot your password next time. You can simply click next to by-pass password. You can reset password later in control panel.

6. Click **Next**, type the name you want to identify your computer with. Choose a desktop picture by clicking on your choice.

7. Click **Next**. Click on the bigger green shield icon to go to the next screen of review date and time.

8. Select by clicking on the arrow down near the time clock.

Once you choose your time zone, Windows automatically sets the date and time correctly. You can reset the time yourself if you want to practice how to by clicking inside the box to highlight the hour, and clicking on the arrow down or up to choose the time. Do the same with the minutes. You can type the time without using the arrow down. Just delete the default time; type the correct hour and minutes.

9. Click **Next**. Click the location where your system is, e.g. home. Click **Next**. And Windows Vista installation says Thank you.

Remember to remove the installation CD. As Windows completes the last configuration, it educates you on its capability to enhance performance. It ends at the login screen if you set a password earlier. If you did not, it goes to your desktop screen ready for you to work. You will have to install other programs and applications if you did a fresh installation. Do the updates after you setup the Internet.

If for instance, you want to download a hardware driver, go to the website of the computer maker. Click on the technical support menu and select drivers and you will be asked to type in your computer's serial number. This information helps the vendor to identify your system and redirect you to the right webpage.

B: Windows XP with Service Pack 3 is the second tutorial. The installation is self-explanatory once you get going.

1. Insert the original Windows CD that came with your computer into the CD-ROM drive. The drive is usually drive D. (If you don't have the CD, buy a copy of Windows XP.

2. Turn off your computer and wait for few seconds. Turn it on. (Another way to do this process is to just restart the computer without completely shutting it down).

3. Tap on **F12** on the keyboard three times when the vendor logo appears on the screen; a vendor logo is for example, HP label.

During this power-on-self-test (POST), Tapping F12 redirects the system to the **Boot Device Menu**. Here the setup asks you what you want to do with the available choices. Note that the mouse will not work on this setup page for now. Use the arrow up and down on the keyboard.

4. Select the **Onboard** or **USB CD-ROM drive** and press **Enter**.

Ignore the next screen that says Press **any key to boot from CD**, if you shutdown the computer before rebuilding. The enter command already takes care of this. This screen appears briefly. If you press a key on the keyboard, the system will boot to Windows and discontinue with the installation. It would think you changed your mind. But if you are rebuilding within the previous Windows installation by restarting, then press any key as asked.

5. The setup asks you to wait and then brings up the license agreement screen. Press **F8** to agree.

It does the initialization by copying files until it gets to the welcome to setup page. It prompts you to press **R** if you want to repair Windows XP, press **C** to install Windows XP or press **F3** to quit.

6. Press **C** to continue.

The setup verifies that your computer meets the system requirement. Then it asks which partition you want to install Windows XP, showing you the storage options with the capacity of each. The master boot record is the main storage which is C: partition 1. NTFS (New Technology File System). NTFS was originally designed for Windows NT. It is been used for other versions since then. Charles Kozierok explains that:

> "Microsoft created the New Technology File System, or NTFS. The goals behind NTFS were to provide a flexible, adaptable, high-security and high-reliability file system, to help position Windows NT as a "serious" operating system for business and corporate users" (Kozierok para. 2).

Note that some computers have more than one partition. I usually select the largest storage which is C: partition.

7.   Select **C partition**. Press enter.

Windows will warn you that you already have the operating system running on your machine, and installing another copy into the same partition may cause Windows to not function properly. Ignore the warning because the first one will be gone after formatting.

The next screen lets you choose the type of NTFS formatting – **quick**, **full** or **leaving current files system intact**. Formatting wipes out the entire contents on a hard drive in preparation for a new installation, unless you choose the third option.

8.   Highlight your choice and press **F.**

I chose the second option which is the full formatting, even though it takes a longer time (about 20 minutes according to the speed of this computer). Ignore the caution from Windows about deleting all contents in the hard disk because you pressed F.

The next page will say Windows is formatting. You will see the setup is copying files and asking you to wait. You will also see the progress by the incremental percentage up to 100 and yellow color gradually filling up the long bar until formatting completes.

You will see the graphical progression as it goes through the menu of install. It also tells you how many minutes left. You will learn about Windows XP's performance and functionality presented in texts and pictures during this time.

The installation pauses on **Region** and **Language** options screen for you to customize. The mouse starts functioning at this stage. If you do not need to change the language or region,

8.   Click **Next**. Setup will continue and pause at personalizing your software.

9.   Type in your name and your organization.

10. Type in your computer name and administrator's password when prompted.

Skip the network domain information if you are installing on a standalone computer. You can also skip the administrator's password if you want your system to boot to Windows without asking for a password. You can set a password later from the control panel under user account.

Many computer owners like to have administrator's password for security reasons. It is recommended. Your system will not boot to Windows without putting in the password you set. This prevents an unauthorized person to get to your files and documents. Microsoft Corporation is very diligent in security matters. It protects your sensitive and personal information.

11. Setup **Date** and **Time** when asked to.

In a nutshell, Windows will prompt you to select or type in information when it needs it until the installation completes. It explains what the promptings mean, e.g. the name of your network. Let's say you have a wireless router setup in your house, you will supply this information for Windows to set it up on your computer.

When the installation finishes, the system will restart and boot to Windows login screen. It boots to Windows if you did not set administrator's password.

12. Login and install other applications and programs.

You may need to install drivers of some components in your computer. You can download drivers online for free. You can run Windows Update to get the latest versions of software and programs on your computer for free.

13. Laptop on your laps: Health-related

When I place a laptop on my laps for about 30 minutes, I begin to feel the weight and the heat gradually increases making it uncomfortable. I usually get up to place a cushion under my laptop. I thought that was the best solution until I started writing this book and decided to say something about laptop hazard. Not wanting to just write what I experienced, I was curious to know if there has been anything written about this health concern. I did a search on the internet and found several studies done. Indeed, it's not safe to put your laptop on your laps. I learnt that a pillow or any soft pad does not solve but may increase the risk. One wonders why it's called a laptop if it is that dangerous. Like in everything, moderation, caution and adherence to the usage instructions enable safety in the use of technology gadgets.

- Laptop got its name from placing the small computer on your laps. It is mobile and lightweight. But it gets heated gradually and you feel it.

- Placing the laptop on the laps was not a big concern in the past as they were not frequently used. Today, notebooks are popular. it is recommended to place a laptop on a hard surface, e.g. a desk; especially if you are using it for a long period of time.

- Due to heat and health issues, notebook placemats are designed and sold in computer stores.

Research studies highlight the danger of overheated laptops on the laps. Here are a few notable findings: From Dr Yefim Sheynkin, Associate Professor of Urology and Director, Male Infertility and Microsurgery:

"Until further studies provide more information on this type of thermal exposure", he said, "teenage boys and young men may consider limiting their use of LC on their laps, as long-term use may have a detrimental effect on their reproductive health." (Sheynkin para. 13).

I suggest reading more from Sheynkin:
http://www.medicalnewstoday.com/articles/17664.php

From Chair of the Mobile Telecommunications and Health Research Program, Professor Lowrie Challis is another educative article:

"That until more research had been carried out, children who used wi-fi enabled laptops should only do so if they kept a safe distance from their embedded antennas….With a desktop computer, the transmitter will be in the tower…This might be perhaps 20cms from your leg and the exposure would then be around one per cent of that from a mobile phone…However if you put a laptop straight on your lap and are using wi-fi, you could be around 2cms from the transmitter, and receiving comparable exposure to that from a mobile phone…Children are much more sensitive than adults to a number of other dangers, such as pollutants like lead and UV radiation, so if there should be a problem with mobiles, then it may be a bigger problem for children." (Challis para. 5, 6, 7, 8, 9).

See more information from Challis and some researchers at
http://www.telegraph.co.uk/news/uknews/1549944/Warning-on-wi-fi-health-risk-to-children.html

I had not seen the effects laptops on laps have on women as I did not do an in-depth search. It is very likely there is. Although the above two references refer to male and children, the danger from the heat can affect anybody. Overheated battery, for instance can cause harm to male and female. More research is going on about technology and health.

14. Wet keyboard

We incidentally spill coffee on our keyboard. Wipe dry immediately to prevent stickiness. If it is a large liquid spill, turn the keyboard face down and let it dry well.

15. Dirty keyboard

Particles wedge in-between the keys. Coupled with dust from the environment, our keyboards can look gross. Dust your keyboard once in a while. You can buy a dust removal meant for keyboards and electronic equipment in computer stores. It is a can of air spray that easily blows out the dust and hidden particles. An example is Dust Off that is a multi-purpose duster. Blow off the dust on your computer too. Canned air spray is safe; here is an informative explanation:

> "The air used for canned air is not the same as the air we all breathe. The mixture is often made up of nitrogen and other harmless gases. It is also known to be ozone safe, which is always good. Now, even though canned air is safe to use on your computer, etc., you do need to pay attention to the kind you buy. A wonderful WorldStart reader informed me that there are two types of canned air: flammable and non-flammable. The can will clearly say whether it's flammable or not, so make sure you read the label closely. If a certain propellant in the canned air mixes with a high voltage from your computer, it could cause flames." (Erin para. 1, 2).

16. Cleaning your monitor screen

Use a damp, lint-free cloth to wipe clean your monitor. Gently wipe it in a circular motion. If you press too hard on the flimsy surface, it dents the screen. You cannot see image or text on the damaged spot. Water or electronic solvent are best for cleaning.

17. If you cannot connect to the Internet

- Check the phone cable if it is a dialup; sometimes the phone cable is loosed. Also, verify that it is plugged into the correct jack. Dialup ports on your computer usually come in pairs. One is labeled "LINE" which is what you want to plug into and the other usually has an icon that looks like a phone. That jack is for hooking up an external phone if you wish to.

- Is it a wireless network? Check the network configuration. Be sure the physical wireless switch (if it's a laptop) is turned to on. You may need to re-scan for the wireless access point. You may type in a security code called WEP (Wired Equivalent Privacy) in some access points to recognize yours if the access point has extra security configured.

- If you type the WEP incorrectly, you may be connected to the access point but would be unable to access the internet. Restart the computer to refresh the access point listing. Type in the correct WEP.

- Note that having a wireless adapter does not automatically give you a wireless internet. You must be in a location that has a wireless access point that is connected to the internet.

- Do you have a LAN (Local Area Network) connection? Check the Ethernet cable; see that the light is on in the network port on the back of the computer. Unplug the cable and plug it in again.

- In many cases, an Ethernet cable may get confused with a phone cable. An Ethernet cable end is wider than a phone cable end and has 8 pins (RJ-45), whereas, a phone cable end has only 2, 4 or 6 pins (RJ-11).

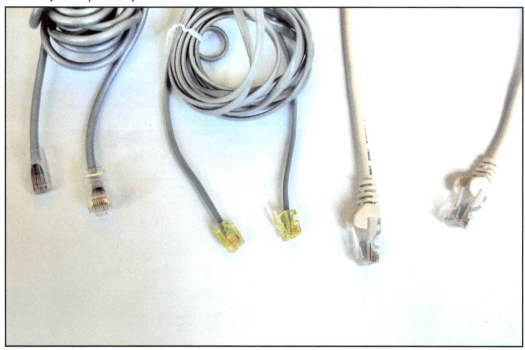

Let's troubleshoot a wireless network problem that is most common in homes and small businesses.

1. Right-click on the wireless icon (two monitors) on the taskbar.

2. Select **Diagnose and repair**. (**Repair** in Windows XP).

3. This will open to Windows Network Diagnostic. The diagnostic will run indicating **identifying the problem...**

4. Windows completes the diagnostic and reports that it successfully fixed the problem. Close and restart your browser. If Windows is unable to repair the problem, try this next step in Chapter 18. (Windows does suggest some solutions).

18. Troubleshooting a high speed internet device using a soft reset method

After you tried the software troubleshooting of connection issue in Chapter 17 with no success, attempt the hardware device repair. Motorola™ wireless modem/DSL is our illustrated device:

1. Use the tip of a pencil or pen to insert into the reset hole on your router to reset it. This soft reset will power off the device to recycle the configuration and restart. This can cause a full system reset back to the factory defaults in some routers/modems.

2. You will see the power turns on and blinks red until it becomes solid green.

3. Then the Ethernet light comes on blinking red and turns solid green. Next is the Wireless light, followed by the DSL light, ending with the Internet light. This is also dependant on which router you have.

4. Close your browser and reopen it. It may take up to five minutes. You should be connected. If not, do the Advanced repair in chapter 19.

Note: Some modems have Phone light and Activity light. The internet or Activity light may go blank after the reset if your browser is not opened. Your modem buttons may not necessary be in this order. But it is the same basic cold reset process all routers go through.

19. Advanced repair of a broadband modem or router using a hard reset method

1. Turn off the power on the router. If there is no on and off button, unplug the power cable. Wait 30 seconds and turn it on.

2. After all the lights turn green, try going online again. If no luck,

3. Unplug the power cable, the Ethernet cable and the phone or DSL cable. (Unplug all the cables connected to the router).

4. Wait for 30 seconds and plug all the cables back starting with the power cable.

5. When all the lights turn green, open your browser to see if you are online. If connection problem persists, repeat the steps or go to Chapter 20.

20. Configuring wireless DSL or cable modem using its web interface

If you know the gateway address of your modem, skip to number 4. (The gateway address is written on the back of the wireless Motorola DSL modem used here. But I still want to feature the IP configuration tool for those who may need it).

1. Open the **Command (cmd) Prompt** window by going to **Start**, **All Programs**, **Accessories** and clicking on **Command Prompt**. Here is what you will see:

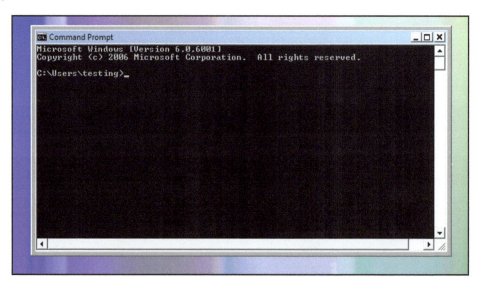

Microsoft product screen shot of Windows Vista ® reprinted with permission from Microsoft Corporation

2. If the cursor is not blinking at the angle bracket > click once near it and type **ipconfig**. Press **Enter**. (Like this, >ipconfig).

This will open the wireless configuration summary:

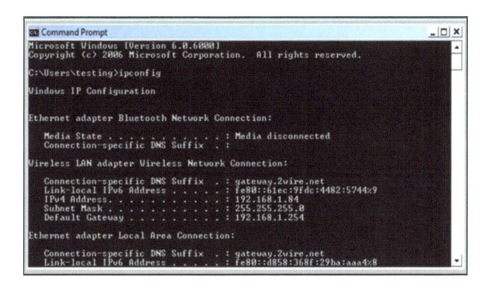

Microsoft product screen shot of Windows Vista ® reprinted with permission from Microsoft Corporation

3. Write down the Default Gateway Address as displayed: 192.168.1.254

4. Open your browser. Clear the URL in the address box and type in the default gateway address you wrote down. Press **Enter** or click the arrow. (Older versions of Internet Explorer have **Go**).

Microsoft product screen shot of Windows Internet Explorer 8 ® reprinted with permission from Microsoft Corporation

The browser opens to a connection information page on the web interface of your high speed internet device. It also displays the ISP's logo of your DSL modem. This does not mean that you are connected to the internet and ready to browse. The web interface is simply a utility, an online Troubleshooting instructions that the ISP walks you through. You too can use the web interface instructions to fix your internet anytime without calling your ISP.

5. See if your user ID (Login username) shows in the **User ID** field. If it is the provider's default user ID, your login will not work. So click on the + sign near **Advanced** on the left menu to expand it. Click on **Connection Configuration**. Type your user ID and password. Repeat the password if prompted. Scroll down and click **Save Changes**.

6. **Access Code Required** page opens. This refers to the modem's 10-digit media access code. Type it in. (Find the access code on the back of the DSL

modem). Click Ok. The configuration takes you back to the previous page. Scroll down and click **Save Changes**. Watch your wireless device buttons as their lights turn solid green. Close the browser and reopen it. Saving changes may automatically reopen the browser and connects you to the internet.

If you still cannot get on the internet, repeat step 4 and 5, but do not click on save changes just yet. Instead scroll to **Let LAN use Public IP Address** under modem information. Click **Yes**. Click **Save Changes**. Restart. The configuration will restart the browser. You should be online when the browser opens to your home page. Call your ISP if the problem persists.

Note: There are different DSL and cable modems; your configuration may be slightly different from some of the above steps. Check the help menu or manual on the online connection information page. Consult the hardcopy manual too.

21. Reconnecting your laptop after a trip

We often travel with our laptops and they may not connect to our network automatically when we return home.

1. Right-click on the wireless icon on the taskbar. It brings up a menu. If you do not see the wireless icon on the taskbar, go to **Start**, **Connect To** and it takes you to the same menu.

2. Click on **Connect to a network**. It opens up available networks with the signal range in your area. Look for yours, click to highlight it.

3. Click on **Connect**. It will ask for SSID (Service Set Identifier). Type it in. SSID is the name of your network. You will be prompted for the WEP (Wired Equivalent Privacy) key. Type it.

4. Setup completes the process and ends at "You are successfully connected to the network."

I have often gone to help people fix their wireless connection. When I ask them for the router's passed, they have no clue what I'm talking about. When I explain what a network key is, the instinctive response is "They didn't give it to me." "They installed the wireless themselves." Next time your ISP setup your network, ask them for the WEP.

- WEP is a 10, 16 or 58 character key configured in your router. If you do not have this privacy key, read the operations guide for the router or call your provider. When you get it, save it for keeps. I wrote mine down. You can save yours on a flash drive.

- You will need the WEP in order to access your wireless network. You may randomly be disconnected from your Broadband wireless network due to some obvious reasons like inclement weather, connectivity issues with ISP communication to your router, your own computer problems. You can reconnect using your WEP, even when you buy a new system.

- WEP is your unique network identifier which is a password that unlocks your wireless device. Think of it as the key to the door of your house. If you do not give out your key, nobody can unlock the door. So also no one can connect to your network if they do not know your network key.

- WEP is the password that secures your wireless from people connecting to it arbitrarily. If you have a guest that wants to connect his or her laptop, type the WEP and the guest will be connected.

22. How to block Spam Emails and unwanted email addresses

In this age of instant messaging, online chats, blogs and emailing, unwanted emails come to a user's inbox, in spite of filters used by ISPs (Internet Service Providers). When a spammer changes just one word in an email address, the filter sees it as a different address and lets it pass through. Some ISPs call unwanted emails junk or spam. By fencing off the spammer's IP (Internet Protocol) address from the Internet Headers, you nip it in the bud. So, block spam emails from coming into your inbox.

Many email accounts have a spam folder on the menu. You can easily click the box near a spam email and click the spam folder which will automatically place the email into the spam folder. You may be asked if you are sure. Another option is to drag and drop the email into the spam folder.

Here are a couple of examples of blocking junk email.

Microsoft Outlook 2007 Email users

1. Right-click on the junk email you received.

2. Select **Message Options**.

3. Highlight the **Originating IP** address (highlight only the numbers/dots, for example, 198.168.3.1).

4. Right-click on it and select **Copy.**

Be careful to not select your provider's IP address or friends and family's email addresses. It is safer to select originating IP address. Some smart spammers configure junk email to purportedly come from your legitimate email provider IP address. If you want to select Received From… select the IP address or the domain name service (DNS) that is unknown to you. You may ask your ISP what its IP address is.

5. Click **Close**; go back to the email, right-click and select **Junk Email.**

6. Scroll to **Junk Email Options**, Select **Blocked Senders.**

7. Click **Add**, right-click inside the box and click **Paste.**

8. Click **Ok.**

9. Click **Apply** and **Ok.** (Courtesy of Microsoft ® Outlook 2007. 1/6/09.)

Yahoo! email users:

1. Login to your Yahoo! email.

2. Click on **Options**; click on **Mail Options.**

3. Click on **Spam Protection.**

4. In **Spam**, select your choice to immediately delete or save messages to Spam Folder.

To block email addresses, follow steps 1 to 3 then

1. Click on **Block Addresses.**

2. Type in the address or copy and paste it.

3. Click **Add block.**

You can unblock it later if you want. (Courtesy of Yahoo!® Mail. 1/7/09).

Hotmail users:

1. Login to Hotmail and click on **Options**. This brings up a table of colors.

2. Click on **More Options.**

3. Click on **Safe and Blocked Senders.**

4. Click on **Blocked Senders**; type in the email address.

5. Click **Add to List**.

This will automatically save the email address to the blocked list and you will stop getting emails from that sender. (Courtesy of Hotmail ®. 1/15/09).

AOL email users:

1. Login to your AOL email.

2. Click on **Settings**, and it opens to **General Settings**.

3. Click on **Spam Controls**; choose from the options; for instance, "Allow mail from only the people I know".

When you are done with how you want spam filters to work for you, go to the menu on the left:

1. Click on **Filters**. If you have not created any filters, AOL will ask you to **Create Filter.** It is a hyperlink that you click on that takes you to the next window and start creating your filters.

2. Fill in the boxes. It is pretty easy to follow - Name your filter; under the **To**, **From**, **Subject**, **Cc**, **Bcc** and **Message Body Contains**, type in the address of that annoying junk email you get frequently.

Note that you do not have to fill in the Cc and Bcc boxes. Cc stands for a copy of the email to another person and the name is visible to the main recipient. Bcc is a blind copy of the email to a person that the main receiver and Cc person will not see or know this person got a copy of the email.

3. Under **Then Move To**, select the folder in the drop-down menu; e.g. spam folder.

4. Click **Create**. AOL takes you to the summary page where you can see your creation. If you click on it, you can edit it. (Courtesy of AOL ® Mail. 1/15/09).

If you use Juno, Gmail, or other service providers, look for options to configure blocking junk emails. Some providers call it user preferences or settings.

23. To turn off a red x that appears instead of a picture on an internet web page.

1. Go to **Tools** in Internet Explorer and scroll down to **Internet Options**.

2. Click on the **Advanced** tab.

3. Under **Multimedia** file look for a list of checked boxes and find **Show Pictures** and check it.

You can right-click on the red x when it comes up on a web page. Deleting it will not stop it reappearing next time. What makes the red x appear is that you do not have the program that the picture was formatted with; you do not have flash or java software installed. It could also be that for security reasons, the firewall from your internet service provider denies the picture from opening for fear of viruses.

24. Uncheck Security Center alert that keeps popping up and annoying you

1. Go to **Start** and navigate to **Control Panel** to open it.

2. Look for **Security Center** and double-click it.

3. On the **Resources** button, click **Change the way security center alerts me**.

4. Uncheck all boxes in the **Alert Settings** screen.

25. Reduce the size of pictures and documents before attaching them to emails

It is highly recommended to compress pictures, huge documents and images attached to emails. Email servers may drop them if they take too long to download. For instance, a 25.6 MB picture is way too big for FTP (file transport protocol) to process during the time it takes to transport it to a sender, and when the sender is downloading it.

a. save the pictures or documents.

b. remember the *name* of the file, and the location where it is saved, e.g., **My Document**.

c. There are several editing software options available to re-size a huge file. Install your choice on your computer before editing.

Take Adobe Photoshop® for instance:

1. Right-click on the picture (best saved picture format is JPEG).

2. Select **Open With** and choose **Other Programs**.

3. Select **Photoshop**, click on **Image** and **Image Size**.

4. Under **Document Size**,

   a. Type 5.097 in the **Height** box and it automatically changes the **Width** to 3.708.

   b. Type 72 in the **Resolution** box. You will notice the width changes to 267 pixels and height 367 pixels in **Pixels Dimensions**.

5. Click **Ok**; go to **File** and click **Save As**; name it and click **Save**; then you can attach it to an email. (Adobe Photoshop ®).

6. The recipient enlarges the image to its normal size by opening and clicking on it. Each click increases the size. (If it gets too large spreading out on the screen, you can click **Undo** or **Zoom Out** to shrink the size).

7. The receiver can use the **Zoom** feature to enlarge an attachment. Open the attachment, right-click on it, click on **Zoom In**. Keep zooming in to the size you want. You can zoom out to decrease the picture or document.

Note: you can go directly to Photoshop to edit; that is, open Photoshop; click on File, Open, look for and highlight your saved file, double click it. It opens inside Photoshop. Click on Image, Image Size and continue with step 4 and 5 above.

26. The best place to get help while on a program or application

1. Click **Help** on top of the menu in the application you are on. Some applications have a question mark icon, e.g. Microsoft Word 2007. See the question mark at the far right corner in the picture below.

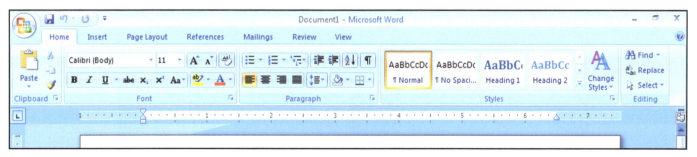

Microsoft product screen shot of Word 2007 ® reprinted with permission from Microsoft Corporation

2. Click on the question mark icon and type a question or topic in the search box, if the default questions are not relevant to yours. This is true for all the applications in Microsoft Office 2007 program.

27. The quickest way to highlight a large document or long list.

1. Highlight the first item by clicking and holding down the mouse while dragging the mouse across it.

2. Scroll to the last item.

3. Hold down the **Shift** key and click once. All contents will be highlighted.

28. The quickest way to delete large files and emails at once.

1. Highlight the first file. (See Chapter 27).

2. Scroll to the last file. Hold down the **Shift** key and click once. This function highlights all files.

3. Click **Delete**.

29. How to copy and paste - 3 options

Option #1: In Microsoft Word 2003 ®, click on **Edit, Select All, Copy**. Go to a new site to paste the copy. Click on the site, and on **Edit**, click on **Paste**. (Or, at that point, simply right-click and select **Paste**).

Option #2: Highlight the contents, hold down the **Ctrl** key and press **C**; click on where to paste it; hold down the **Ctrl** key, and press **V**.

Option #3: This is a drag and drop function. Minimize both documents, the source of the copy as well as the site of the paste, so you can see both pages at the same time. Click and hold down the mouse to highlight the contents of the copy, and do not let go; while still holding down the mouse drag the contents to the page where it will be pasted. Release the mouse.

Note: Microsoft Office 2007 ® makes it easier to do cut and paste as there are cut and paste icons in the **Home** button at the top of the page. The icons are grayed out by default. Once a text is highlighted, the icons lit up.

30. How to cut and paste

This is similar to copy and paste.

1. **Edit**, **Select All**, **Cut**. Go to where you want it pasted.

2. Click on **Edit**, click on **Paste**.

3. To use the keyboard instead, hold down the **Ctrl** key, press the **X** key.

4. Go to the page to paste it, hold down the **Ctrl** key and press **V**.

31. How to take a screenshot.

1. Press **Print Screen** key on the keyboard.

2. Open word processor e.g. Microsoft Word 2007, hold down the **Ctrl** key, press **V**. It will paste the content of the screen on the page.

3. Then print or save the screenshot.

32. Configure your desktop as start menu or classic start menu

"Classic start menu is the style that gives the look and functionality of previous versions of Windows. The Start menu provides easy access to your folders, favorite programs and search." (Microsoft Windows Vista ®).

Classic Start Menu screen in Windows XP   Start Menu screen in Windows XP

Microsoft product screen shots of Windows XP® reprinted with permission from Microsoft Corporation

In Windows XP

1. Right-click on **Start** button; select **Properties**, and it opens to **Start Menu** page, if not click on **Start Menu**.

2. Click on either **Classic Start Menu** or **Start Menu**. If your choice is already setup, do nothing.

3. Click **Apply** and **Ok**.

In Windows Vista

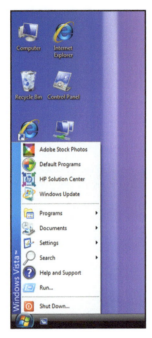 

Classic Start Menu screen in Windows XP   Start Menu screen in Windows XP

Microsoft product screen shots of Windows XP® reprinted with permission from Microsoft Corporation

1. Right-click on **Start** button and select **Properties**. Click on **Start Menu** if the page did not default to it.

2. Click on **Classic Start Menu** or **Start Menu**. It depends on your choice.

3. Click **Apply** and **Ok**. If your choice is already setup, do nothing.

33. Enlarge the desktop screen fonts so you can see better

A. In Windows XP

It is quicker to get to the Display settings by right-clicking on your (plain) desktop and selecting Properties. Then continue from number 2. But if you want to configure your desktop without having to minimize your opened applications to make room for a plain space, start from number 1.

If this is your screen: go to **Start**, click on **Control Panel**

Microsoft product screen shot of Windows XP® reprinted with permission from Microsoft Corporation

If this is your screen: go to Start, click on **Settings** and **Control Panel**.

Microsoft product screen shot of Windows XP® reprinted with permission from Microsoft Corporation

1. Navigate to **Display** icon, and double-click it. Select **Settings**

2. Under **Screen Resolution** drag the bar to 800 x 600 pixels

3. Click **Apply**. The screen will go blank for few seconds and back to ask if you want the new setting. Click Yes. Click **Ok**

B.   In Windows Vista:

It is quicker to get to the **Display settings** by right-clicking on your (plain) desktop and selecting **Personalize**). Then continue from number 3. But, if you want to configure your desktop without having to minimize your opened applications to make room for a plain space, start from number 1.

1. If this is your screen: go to **Start**,

Microsoft product screen shot of Windows Vista ® reprinted with permission from Microsoft Corporation

2. Open **Control Panel**, click on **Personalization**.

3. Click on **Display Settings**; in **Resolution**, drag the bar to 800 x 600 pixels.

4. Click **Apply**. The screen will go blank for few seconds and back to ask if you want the new setting. Click **Yes**. Click **Ok**.

1. If this: open **Control Panel**.

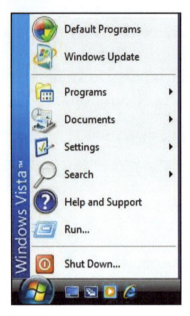

Microsoft product screen shot of Windows Vista ® reprinted with permission from Microsoft Corporation

2. Double-click on **Personalization**. Scroll to **Display Settings**.

3. Under **Resolution**, drag the bar to the size of pixels you want.

4. Click **Apply**. The screen will go blank for few seconds and back to ask if you want the new setting. Click **Yes**. Click **Ok**.

34. Changing the size of icons on the computer screen

1. Go to **Start**, open **Control Panel**, and click on **Personalization** in Windows Vista. (If it's Windows XP, click on Display).

2. Select **Display Settings**, it opens up another screen called **Monitor**. (Windows XP users, select Settings).

3. Under **Resolution**, drag the bar to the size of pixels you want.

4. Drag the bar forward to 1012 x 768 or higher. Click **Apply**. The screen will go blank for few seconds and back to ask if you want the new setting. Click **Yes**. Click **Ok**.

Here is a quicker alternative:

1. Minimize any opened program so only the (plain) desktop is visible

2. Right-click anywhere on the desktop.

3. Select **Properties**, click on **Settings**. (For Windows Vista users, select Personalize).

4. Under **Screen Resolution** drag the bar to 1012 x 768 (or higher); click **Apply**. The screen will go blank for few seconds and back to ask if you want the new   setting. Click **Yes**. Click **Ok**.

35. Creating a short cut on your desktop screen

Create a shortcut for any program or application so you can easily open it without having to go to **Start** and **Program** to look for it. The example here is from Microsoft Word 2007. Close all the opened programs and documents so that only the desktop is visible.

1. Go to **Start**, click on **Programs**, and select **Microsoft Office 2007**.

2. Scroll to **Microsoft Word**. Right-click on it and do not release the mouse until you drag Word icon to the desktop. This function gives you options.

3. Select **Copy Here** or **Create a Shortcut Here**.

36. Closing many opened applications on the taskbar at once

Sometimes we open too many files and documents at the same time and they use up lots of memory which can slow down or freeze the computer

1. Click on one of the programs on the **Taskbar**.

2. Hold down the **Ctrl** key and click the rest. Release the **Ctrl** key.

3. Right-click on any of the selected programs.

4. Choose **Close Group**, and click **Ok**.

37. Lock the taskbar so it does not accidentally move to the sides of the screen.

The default taskbar screen is horizontal and on the bottom. We sometimes find that the start button has moved vertically to the right or left; horizontally to the top. We didn't know how it happened; we didn't know what we touched. Lock it.

1. Right-click on the taskbar. (Be sure to right-click on a free space on the taskbar and not on any icon or opened programs. It is safer to close all opened files.

2. Click on **Lock the Taskbar**.

Note: the taskbar is the long bar that runs from right to left on the bottom of the screen. This is home to the start button and the time including other startup program/application icons.

38. How to place the task bar where it belongs

It can be tricky and tough to return the taskbar to the default place. The taskbar has to be in unlocked state for you to do this configuration.

1. Right-click and hold-down the **Start** button on the taskbar wherever it is.

2. Drag and drop it back to the bottom of the screen.

39. A quick way to reduce a cluttered taskbar

Vendors load many programs and applications on new computers desktops placing them in the startup folder. The abundance installations create icons on the taskbar near the time and start button for visibility and quick launching. You can customize your taskbar to a minimum.

1. Right-click on a free space anywhere on the taskbar.

2. Click on **Tools** and uncheck the items that you do not want.

40. Adding a new taskbar

1. Right-click on the taskbar. (Not on an icon or opened program).

2. Click on **Tools** and select **New Taskbar**.

3. Select from the items and click **Ok**. Create a new folder if needed.

41. Customizing your screen saver to display your own texts

1. Right-click on the desktop screen (be sure it's on a plain desktop).

2. Click on **Properties** (or **Personalize** in Windows Vista).

3. Click **Screen Saver**. Click on the arrow down under screen saver and select **3D Test**.

4. Click on **Settings** and type your text. For instance, Happy Birthday. You can customize the fonts, the motion, surface style, resolution and so on. Click **Ok** when finished.

5. Click **Preview** and it displays your creation; click once to stop it.

6. Click **Apply** if satisfied and click **Ok**. You may set the time the screen saver will start when the computer is idle.

42. Transferring files from an old computer to a new system

A.   *In Windows XP*

1. Click **Start** and select **All Programs**.

2. Scroll to **Accessories**, click on **System Tools**, then **Files and Settings Transfer Wizard**.

3. Click **Next**, select **Old Computer**, click **Next**, **Other** and **Browse**.

4. Expand the + sign in the **My Computer** icon as well as the + sign in the **Local Drive C:**

5. Select **Create a new folder**; name it; e.g. Bob's files.

6. Click **Ok**, **Next**, select **Both Files and Settings**. (This function moves email, etc).

7. Click **Next**, and the wizard starts copying. This takes time, depending on the size of files you have. When this finishes, go to your new PC.

8. In the new computer, repeat step 1 and 2 by Clicking **Start** and selecting **All Programs**, and scrolling to **Accessories**, clicking on **System Tools**, then **Files and Settings Transfer Wizard**.

9. Click **Next** and select **New Computer**, click **Next**, **Other** and **Browse**.

10. Look for the new folder you created, named Bob's files.

11. Highlight it; click **Ok** and the Wizard transfers the files to the new computer.

B.   In Windows Vista

1.   Click **Start** and select **All Programs**.

2.   Scroll to **Accessories**, and click on **System Tools**.

3.   Look for **Windows Easy Transfer**; follow the onscreen instructions.

Note: The startup welcome page is another location of the windows easy transfer tool. You can also transfer files by simply buying a transfer cable that connects both old and new computers for the process. Transfer file cables can be found in a Computer store.

43. To move a picture to the desired location on a page

You may insert a picture and you find that it is not in the right position, e.g. too far to the left margin. You can click on it and drag to the location. Sometimes, dragging does not work. Do the following:

1.   Click on the picture

2.   Hold down the **Ctlr** key and press the **Space bar** key. Release the **Ctlr** key.

3.   Hold down the **Space bar** key and use the **Arrow down** key to bring the cursor to the image. The cursor should be blinking now.

4.   Begin clicking on the **Space bar** key and the image will be moving until it gets to where you want it. You can also use the Arrow keys.

44. When you unintentionally hold down the Shift key for too long

Many times we find that we have absent mindedly pressed a key. It executes a command and something goes wrong with our typing. We often exclaimed, "Gosh; I don't know what I did." This happened to me. I was deep in thoughts about the next words to write with my fingers poised on the keyboard ready to type. I must have pressed the Shift key and held it down. All of a sudden a message popped up on the screen prompting me about something. Not wanting to lose my train of thoughts I just clicked x without thinking about it.

What happened? When I started to type, it all turned into caps. Yet, the caps lock light was not on. I pressed the caps lock to unlock it thinking I must have locked it somehow. My typing turned into all lower case, even when I wanted an upper case. Whatever key I pressed, the keyboard gave me the opposite of what I wanted.

I didn't have time for this, why it happened and how to resolve it. I was getting impatient.

To save myself from frustration, I simply closed my work and reopened it. This disabled the command and returned the keyboard to normal.

The outcome of holding down the shift key for 8 seconds

Microsoft product screen shot of Windows Vista ® reprinted with permission from Microsoft Corporation

45. Tapping the Shift key 5 times

You may just be tapping on a key without realizing you are prompting the keyboard to execute a command. It's like chewing on your pencil or drumming on the keyboard with your fingers while your thoughts are far away. I had pressed a key unknowingly and each subsequent word I type deletes the previous one. Very annoying. I usually just close the document and reopen it. I get calls from frantic users about such issues. I would say calm down, you are not alone. It happens to me too. You can hear the relief in their voice. I was distracted one day by something and I kept tapping the shift key and this window popped up:

The result of pressing the shift key 5 times

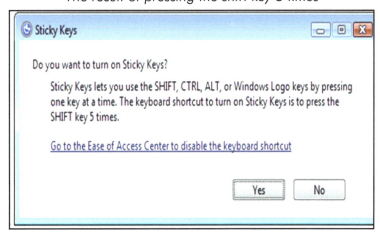

Microsoft product screen shot of Windows Vista ® reprinted with permission from Microsoft Corporation

I said to myself, "Ooh, there we go again." I was patient to read the entire message this time and I clicked No. "Thank you. My mistake!" Press the shift key five times and click on Go to the Ease of Access Center to disable the keyboard shortcut. There you will find other customizations such as disabling the keyboard sound so it doesn't click, click, click when you type.

46. Where to find the amount of memory your system has

Windows Vista has the system memory information on its Welcome Center at startup. If you uncheck **Run at Startup**, the screen will not show the next time you computer boots to Windows. Locate the memory site in Control Panel and click on **System Maintenance** or do following:

1. Right-click on **Computer** icon. (**My Computer** in Windows XP).

2. Click on **Properties**.

3. Under **System**, scroll to **Memory (RAM)** and you will see the amount of memory, e.g. **2046 MB** or **2.00 GB Ram**.

   - The capacity translates to 2 Gigs of memory which is an average speed compared to 4-Gigs of memory.

   - When you open many files, your computer will just crawl if you have only **890 MB** which is less than one gig. Each opened file uses up memory including other system processes running invisibly. This situation does not enhance multi-tasking. Smooth and high performance multi-tasking is a goal of Windows operating systems beginning with Windows 95.

   - Although some programs are allocated virtual memory, the more physical memory your computer has, the faster you navigate different screens, websites and open and close documents. An instance is opening a PDF file which in itself is slow due to its huge file format. If the computer memory is small, it takes awhile to open or print.

47. Locating the speed of your computer

Windows Vista has computer information on its **Welcome Center** at startup. If you uncheck **Run at Startup** in welcome center, the screen will not display it the next time your computer boots to Windows. Get the system information in **Control Panel** and click on **System Maintenance** or do the following:

1. Right-click on **Computer** icon. (**My Computer** icon in Windows XP)

2. Click on **Properties**.

3. Scroll to **Processor** under **System** and you will see **2.20 GHz**, for instance. 2.20 GHz is a fast chip.

   - If the processor is in MB as with older computers, it means your computer is slow. A processor is not a component you easily change or upgrade. Although it's upgradeable, the chip is very delicate with tiny pins that must fit correctly into the socket. If placed wrongly, they can bend and will not work.

   - System information screen is also where you find the maker of your chip, besides the pasted logo on your PC or inside your laptop. The chip maker could be Intel or AMD. You will see if your computer has 32-bit or 64-bit operating system. 64-bit is mostly for newer systems and it's faster with a higher performance and optimization.

48. Checking the strength of the signal in your wireless connection

   - Point to the wireless icon to verify your system is connected to your own wireless network. (It is an icon of two monitors on the far right corner of the taskbar. Some icons are in ascending long green bars).

   - Under **You are currently connected to**, you will see the name of your wireless network. (Be sure it's yours as a computer can pick up a roaming wireless network that is unsecured if yours is faulty or has a very weak signal).

   - Excellent signal will have full solid green bars. You can hardly connect to the internet if it's just two green bars. If you connect at all, your browsing will be slow.

   - To get detailed information and the actual translation of your signal, point the cursor to the icon and double-click it. Select **Network and Sharing Center**. You can also get to this location by right-clicking on the wireless icon and selecting **Network and Sharing Center**.

   - See the status under **Signal Strength**. You can click on **View Details** near the name of your wireless network to read more.

49. How to download pictures from a camera to a computer

1. Be sure your computer is on and booted to the operating system, e.g. Windows Vista. Plug the tiny endpoint of the USB (Universal Serial Bus) cable that came with the camera to the tiny camera port. Then plug the other end to the computer USB port.

2. Turn on the camera. Select computer on your camera if prompted. Windows automatically detects the new hardware and installs it. If not, install the camera software first.

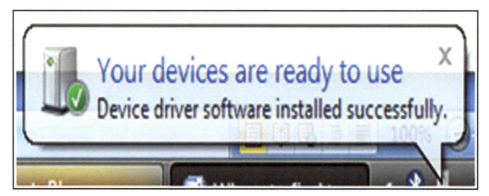

Microsoft product screen shot of Windows Vista ® reprinted with permission from Microsoft Corporation

3. Auto play opens picture options for you to select the next line of action. Click on **Open folders to view files**.

Microsoft product screen shot of Windows Vista ® reprinted with permission from Microsoft Corporation

4. Double-click on **DCIM** (Digital Camera Images); the numbering of the pictures starts with 101MSDCF. Double-click the **101MSDCF** folder to open the pictures. (Some cameras show their own image. You may open My Computer and double-click the camera to open it).

5. The options of what to do next are on the menu. Highlight all the pictures and save, burn to CD, print, publish on the website, view as a slide show or email.

50. **Check your wireless network to see if it is secured**

- Some people do not lock their wireless network and anybody within its range can connect to it. Too many connections weaken the signal and expose the PC to viruses and illegal activities such as hackings. This can also result in your ISP disconnecting your service. You are responsible for everything that connects through your wireless router, so protect it!

- If your internet provider installs your network, they usually secure it. To know if yours is locked:

1. Right-click on the wireless icon on the taskbar. Click **Connect to a network**. (If you do not see the wireless icon on the taskbar, go to **Start, Connect To** and it takes you to the same menu).

2. Look for the name of your wireless router/access point and see if it has a padlock or plain monitor as in Windows Vista. Padlock or plain monitor

indicates the wireless is locked and secured. Windows operating system states clearly whether a network is secured or not. See the screenshot below:

Microsoft product screen shot of Windows Vista ® reprinted with permission from Microsoft Corporation

51. How to lock your wireless network.

Do the following if Windows displays your network is unsecured:

1. Right-click on the wireless icon on the taskbar. It brings up a menu. If you do not see the wireless icon on the taskbar, go to **Start**, **Connect To** and it takes you to the same menu.

2. Click on **Connect to a network**. It opens up available networks within the range of your area. Look for yours, click to highlight it.

Microsoft product screen shot of Windows Vista ® reprinted with permission from Microsoft Corporation

3. Click on **Connect**. It will prompt for some information e.g. SSID (Service Set Identifier). Type it in. SSID is the name of your network. Type the WEP (Wired Equivalent Privacy) key. (See chapter 21).

4. Setup completes the process and ends at "You have successfully completed your network setup." Remember your WEP for next time use.

52. Use your own picture as your desktop background

The fastest customization is to right-click on the picture and select set as my desktop. To go the long route:

In Windows Vista

1. Right-click on the plain desktop and select **Personalize**.

2. Click on **Desktop Background**. It defaults to Windows Wallpapers in the **Picture Location** box. Click on the arrow down to select **Pictures**.

3. Click on **Browse**. Windows will open the picture folder.

4. Double-click on the picture you want and it will automatically save it among the desktop display properties.

5. Click on the picture to highlight. Click on the circle besides one of the display formats of your choice.

6. Click **Ok**. Close the Personalize window. And you will see your picture on your screen. If you want to undo it, go back to the display background and repeat the process.

In Windows XP

1. Right-click on the plain desktop and select **Properties**.

2. Click on **Desktop** and on **Browse**.

3.   Windows will open **My Picture** folder. Double-click on the picture you want. Windows will save it to the display folder.

4.   Click on the picture to highlight it if it is not automatically highlighted.

5. Click on the arrow down besides the position box – stretch, tile or center. As you select Windows shows you the preview.

6. Choose the color of your choice by clicking on the arrow down under **Colors**. Click on the color you selected and you will see the preview.

7. When you are satisfied click on **Apply** and **Ok**. Your desktop screen will display your picture. You can change the picture by repeating the process. That will replace your present picture as you cannot delete a picture from the display folder.

53. How to disable unwanted programs automatically running at startup.

New computers these days come loaded with all kinds of software, tools, games and ads. The contents are configured to open at startup, that is, when you boot to the operating system. Their icons clutter the taskbar and the screen.

- I ask users if they need some of the features I see on their desktops and the reply is "I don't even know what they are."

- Well here is a way to put on hold the programs you do not use. It is not a deletion. You just disable them from starting up when computer boots to Windows. You can always open such programs from Start and All Programs. Remember you can enable the files if you want them at startup.

- The procedure is an advanced technical setting but you can do it. You are smart enough. That is the purpose of this book. You can out-smart the annoying ads. Am I trying to build your confidence or what? Yep, I am.

1. Go to **Start**, click on **Run** and type **msconfig**. If using Windows Vista type msconfig in the **Search** box.

2. Click **Ok**. Windows takes you to **System Configuration Utility**.

3. Click on **Startup**. Here begins the expertise you need to know which extension is for what application under **Startup Item**.

Caution, do not uncheck any extension you don't understand what it stands for. Stay away from system file extensions. Helpful is when you drag the bar between **Start Item** and **Command** to expand the contents giving you an idea what each file represents.

To drag the bar, place the mouse between start item and command and when it forms a plus sign, drag the bar to the right. If you are not sure of the meaning of an extension, write it down, go online and Google it. Google will offer many websites to look up the meaning. Microsoft knowledge base does a good job of interpreting file extensions.

4.   You can uncheck **qtask** which stands for quick task. **Yahoo messenger**, **ITunes Helper**, **JSchedule** stands for Java Schedule update.

5.   Once you are done, click **Apply** and **Ok**. The system will prompt you to restart before the change will take place.

6.   Click **Ok** to restart.

7.   After the PC boots to the operating system, a notification box opens alerting you about the change and to click Ok to not display the notification when next you boot to Windows.

8.   Notice the disappearance of the icons that had cluttered your desktop and the taskbar.

You can stop the programs in task manager but they will start again the next time the system boots to Windows. If you choose to, right-click on the taskbar, select **Task Manager** and click on **Processes**. Select one program at a time and click on **End Process**. You will get a warning. Click **End Process**.

54. How to upgrade or replace a bad memory

- First find out the type of memory module in your computer. Let me describe this function in plain English to reduce technical jargons that may confuse you. Each RAM stick has a specific speed, type and number of pins (gold plates at the bottom of the stick).

- Newer desktop/tower computers have DIMMs – DDR SDRAM, DDR2 SDRAM. Laptops usually have SO DIMMs. It may be difficult to find the exact memory type to buy if your computer is older than 7 years. Older PCs have DRAM, SIMM types. As we know computer stores do not sell old stuff!

- You can replace computer memory with a larger capacity type if they fit into the DIMM slot and if the type and speed match. It is important to purchase the same speed, type and number of pins; e.g. 2GB can replace 512 MB in one DIMM slot. You can buy two 2GB if your system has two slots making it 4GB of the same speed.

- Here is an example of a mix-match that will not work: 1GB DDR 566 MHz PC5300 is not compatible with 1GB DDR2 667 MHz PC2 5300. The 566 speed will not work with 667 speed. Same with this obvious mix-match: 2GB 800 MHz DDR2 4300 will not work with 2GB 800 MHz DDR2 5300. Notice the type - 5300 and 4300.

- Know that towers/desktops memory is different from a laptop and printer memory. Towers/desktops memory is twice the length of a laptop and printer memory.

- For your own safety, and the safety of your hardware, it is recommended that you wear an antistatic strap on your wrist. The strap, when used correctly, helps to ground you from electrical shock due to static spark. Whatever you do, be careful to not touch or hold the ram by the gold-plated pins.

- The following pictures illustrate the steps to add memory or replace a bad one:

Laptop (Notebook)

1. Turn off the system, unplug any cables; remove the battery.

2. Place the laptop face down on a hard surface, a table or desk.

3. Locate the spot usually labeled m. If no label, look for where a tiny screw is screwed down in a small compartment. You can check the manual or search your vendor's website to find where the memory is installed. You need the laptop serial number to search online.

4. Use a screw driver (usually Philips) that fits the tiny screw. Unscrew the plate cover and put it aside.

5. Find the tabs that hold the memory in place; use your thumbs to push them apart toward the sides to eject the memory. (Some laptops have one hook which needs to be pulled up). Take out the memory.

6. You will see the information of the memory both inside the DIMM slot and on the memory.

7. Gently slide the new memory into the slot aligning it to fit properly. Note the groove between the gold pins. This should be aligned to the notch in the slot. Do not force it in. Snap into place. If you inserted the ram properly, the tabs will clasp.

This picture on the right shows a notebook with two memory modules

8.   Screw the plate cover back over the memory. Plug in the battery and power adapter. Turn on the notebook. After showing the logo the system will report that the system memory has changed. It will configure the change and then boot to the operating system.

9.   The notebook is ready for use at a faster performance.

Tower and desktop

A PC tower usually has more DIMM slots.

1.   Unplug the power cable from the computer. Open the case. Some cases may have screws which you have to unscrew. The example here is courtesy of a Dell™ Optiplex GX-755 which has a latch you simply pull towards you and it releases the case.

2. Reach for the two edges of the ram stick and push apart the hinges. Remove it. Do so with each ram.

3. Insert the new ram. Once in, the hinges will snap close. If you do not insert the ram well into the socket, the hinges will not latch. Be careful to not force the ram in; it can bend the gold-plated edges. Note the groove between the gold pins. This should be aligned to the notch in the slot.

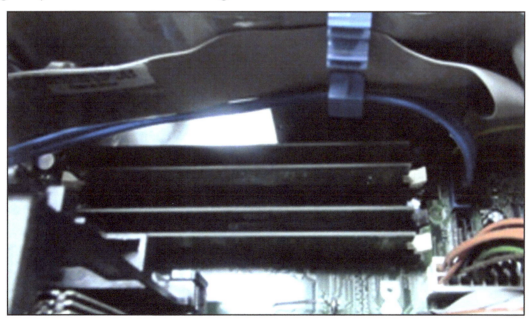

4. Plug in the power cable and turn on the PC. After showing the logo the system will tell you that the system memory has changed. It will configure the change and then boot to the operating system.

5. Once the system is working fine, shutdown it down, unplug the power cable. Put back the case. And you are set to go.

6. Some operating systems such as Windows XP and older, have a 4GB limit. Meaning that if you have 4GB running Windows XP, and depending on your hardware (video/sound cards), Windows will detect less than 4GB.

55. Installing a new hard drive.

- You may want to replace your system's hard drive or add another for increased capacity. It could be the drive crashed. Save your data first in an external storage if you are replacing the drive. (See chapter 10 on how to save on an external storage).

- Open the case to check the type of hard disk cable that is in your system before going to buy a new one. Another location to get this information is from the system bios. Tap F2 three times as soon as the logo shows when you boot up the computer.

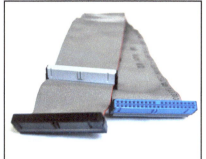 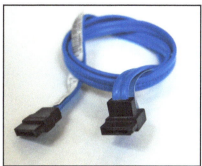 

IDE cable   SATA cable

- Since the IDE or SATA cable connects the hard drive to the connectors on the motherboard, it is wise to buy the right hard drive the cable will match that will match the pins. You have to re-install the operating system.

Tower or Desktop

1. Turn off the system and unplug the power cable. Open the case. Some cases may have screws which you have to unscrew.

Note: If you are only adding a hard drive to the existing one, install it and connect the SATA cable to the drive and the connector on the motherboard. The operating system will recognize it as a second drive.

If it is a drive with an IDE cable ribbon, remove the drive and install the new one in its place if you are replacing the previous drive. If you are only installing an additional drive, use the second connector pins from the existing IDE cable to connect the new one.

- Set the jumper. Use Cable Select (CS) to set jumpers master and slave correctly. Find the CS instruction on the front of the hard drive. Or check the manual. Each hard drive manufacturer, e.g. Maxtor, Seagate or Western Digital has different number of pins that must be set to specifics; if not the bios will not recognize the hard drive.

- A jumper is a tiny rubber tube with a metal lining inside pins of the earlier hard drive technology that denotes primary or secondary drive. The cable select option comes from the manufacturers. This ATA hard drive is found in older computers. Newer computers come in SATA with no jumper settings.

2. If it is a replacement, unplug the hard disk power cable. Disconnect the IDE or SATA cable from the drive. Pull out the drive. Some may be screwed to two brackets inside the computer with four screws. Unscrew them to remove the hard drive.

3. Install the new hard drive. Plug the power cable and close the case. Power on the system.

4. Install the operating system, e.g. Windows Vista. (See chapter 12 on rebuilding a computer).

Notebook

1. Turn off the system, unplug any cables; remove the battery.

2. Place the laptop face down on a hard surface, a table or desk.

Locate the spot usually labeled c. If no label, look for a tiny screw screwed down in a small compartment usually towards the front left edge. You can check the manual or search your vendor's website for the location of the hard drive. You need the laptop serial number to search online.

3. Unscrew the screw using a Philips.

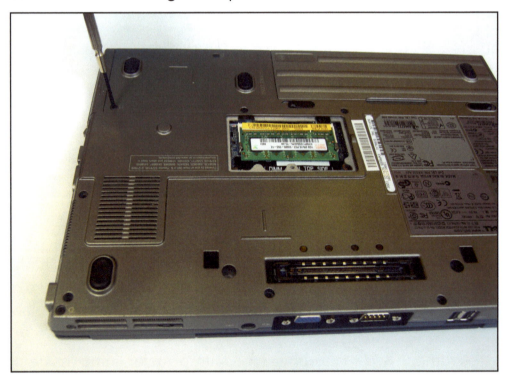

4.   Pull out the hard drive.   Put it aside.

5.   Install the new hard drive turning it face down as in the second picture.

6.   Screw in the screw and insert the battery, plug in the power adapter and turn on the notebook.

7.   Re-install the operating system and other programs. (See chapter 12). Then download your saved data to the new hard drive.

56. Not responding

This is a common error message we see as we work on a document. It could be a game we are playing and it freezes. It is always something that hangs up when we are busy working or when we want to close an application. Here are two ways to close.

A.   Within the data that is not responding

1.   Right click on the plain task bar. Be sure to not click on any icon and opened file. Find any space between the start button and the time.

2. Select **Task Manager**. It will open Windows Task Manager.

3. Click on **Applications**. You will see the application that says **Not Responding**.

4. Click to highlight it. Click on **End Task**.

B.   Using the keyboard

Sometimes trying to close a file freezes up the entire system. You meet with resistance wherever you click on the screen. You click and click, nothing happens; the mouse may even join the freeze, very frustrating. Use the keyboard. It becomes handy as it is not affected. It works outside the unresponsive milieu.

1. Press **Ctlr Alt Del**. It opens up Windows Security screen.

2. Click on **Task Manager** and repeat number 3 and 4 above.

If these two solutions do not close the frozen document or computer, do a force shutdown by pressing and holding the physical power button on the system for few seconds. You may lose your unsaved data.

57. Fdisk formatting

Fdisk is a program used on earlier computers to change or adjust the partitions on the hard drive. Fdisk is still in use especially for older computers hence I featured it here. You need a DOS boot disk to do Fdisk. To create a DOS boot disk, go to: http://www.computerhope.com/boot.htm#02

1. Insert the DOS boot disk; restart, tap **F12** three times as soon as the vendor logo appears. The command redirects the system to Boot Menu. (Some brands of computers may be F10 or so).

2. Select **CD-DVD-R** by pressing the down arrow on the keyboard. You may select **floppy disk** if that is what you have. (The mouse will not work at this stage).

3. Select number **4** to see the number of displayed partitions to delete.

4. Press **Esc** (Escape on the keyboard). Select number **3** that says **Delete......** It opens to option to select from.

5. Select number **4** to delete **Non-DOS**; select the number of the partition starting from ascending number if there is more than one partition.

6. Press **Y** when prompted. (Y is yes and point of no return, data will be lost). Press **Esc**.

7. Select number **3** to delete **Partition or Logical Dos partition**. Select the next partition number, e.g. **1**. Press **Y** when asked. Press **Esc**. (If DOS reports none to delete, press **Esc**). When all the partitions are deleted DOS will open creation dialogue.

8. Select number **1** to create primary partition. Press **Enter**. (To create extended partition, select the number and press enter).

9. Wait for the operating system to prompt for an answer; press **Y**. Press **Esc** when prompted.

10. Press **Ctrl Alt Del** to restart. Press **F12** when the vendor logo appears. Select **CD-DVD-R** drive. Press **Enter** when prompted. (If not, the system will report an error message of "Non-System Disk", because at this stage, there is no graphical operating system, e.g. Windows Vista for the computer to boot to).

11. The system will boot to drive **A:>** then type **Format C:** and press Enter. This is the result, **A:>Format C:**

12. Press **Y** and **Enter** at the alert that all in non-removable drive will be erased.

13. When the formatting completes, press **Enter** for none when prompted. The PC will restart. Press **F12** when the vendor logo appears. Select **CD-DVD-R** drive. Press **Enter** when prompted. It'll boot to the command prompt A:>

14. Type **R:** and press Enter. The result will be **A:>R:**

15. Remove the DOS CD and replace with Windows Vista or Windows XP CD to be installed. That ends the Fdisk procedure.

16. Restart the system by pressing **Ctlr Alt Del**. Once the vendor logo appears, tap **F12** three times to go to **Boot Menu**.

17. Select **CD/DVD-R** drive. Press **Enter**. The operating system will prompt to Press any key to boot from CD or DVD...

18. Press **Enter**. The installation continues. Follow the instructions in **Chapter 12, A or B**. Skip to step **2** since Fdisk already started the installation completing step **1**.

58. Printing

I did not talk about printing. However, the easiest solution to most common printing problems is restarting the printer, though not when it's a paper jam, low toner or ink cartridge. In that case, remove the paper jam and replace the ink cartridge. Some printers require restarting after you solve those two problems.

59. Tidbits

- "Do you want to close all Tabs?" You may have seen this message pops up on your screen when you want to close a web browser. It is a reminder that you have more than one webpage open. Let's say for instance, Yahoo!, Walgreens and Bestbuy WebPages are opened, if you click the red X to close the Bestbuy webpage that you were working on, you get a reminder. In this case make a choice.

When you choose to close all,

1. Click **Yes** to that question;

2. If no, go to the small x on the menu near the left side (not the red X on the right) and click it to close the current webpage.

3. Internet Explorer 8 now adds more options to the pop up: **"Close current tab"**; to **check if you want to "Always close tabs"** without notification.

Note: you can customize the setting if you don't want to be reminded.

1. Right-click on **Internet Explorer**,

2. Click on **Internet Properties**,

3. Scroll down to **Tabs** and click on **Settings** near change how WebPages are displayed in tabs. Check the box on **Warn me when closing multiple tabs**. If you don't want to be notified, uncheck it.

- To use your Laptop with a projector that is already connected to a computer:

Press **Fn** key and the key with a monitor icon on the keyboard, (it is **F8** or **F5** key in some laptops). This is a dual use of a projector. You need a dual VGA (Video Graphical Array) or DVI (Digital Video adapter) to setup this function.

- Have you noticed sometimes when you type, nothing appeared on the page? That is because the mouse is not where it should be. When typing in a box, for instance, your password, click inside the box first to be sure the cursor is blinking inside before you start typing.

- Rather than deleting a URL (Universal Resource Locator is a website address) using the backspace key one by one, highlight it by double-clicking inside the address box. Begin to type the new address and it would delete the previous address. Same goes for texts in a word processor page.

- After typing a website in the URL, press **Enter** rather than using the mouse to click **Go**. It's faster.

- Press **Home** key to take you to the beginning of the line you started typing.

- Press **Home** key and arrow up to take you to the top of the page

60. The anatomy of a computer

These pictures show the anatomy of a computer. A laptop has similar parts but they are smaller. I used to be curious of how inside a computer looks like until I studied systems engineering. Some components are upgradable and replaceable.

Figure 1A: Hard Drive. (Courtesy of Maxtor ™).

Figure 1B: Hard Drive back view.

Figure 2: CD/DVD Drive.

Figure 3: Floppy Drive.

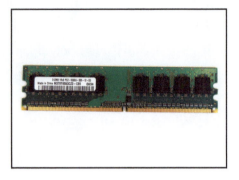

Figure 4: Memory. (RAM stick).

Figure 4B: Ram back view.

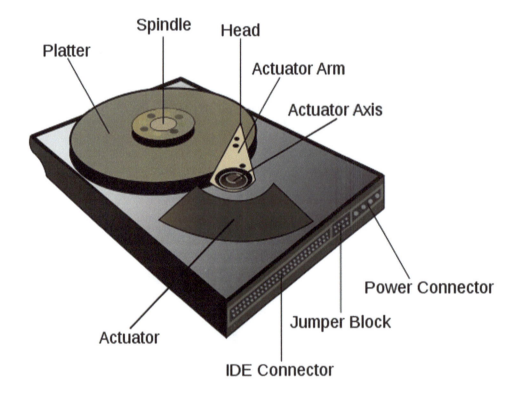

Figure 5: Hard Drive details. (Free para.1).

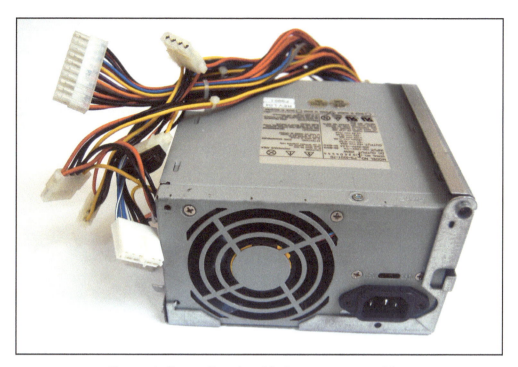

Figure 6: Power Supply with the connector cables.

Figure 7: CPU Fan for ventilation and cooling purposes.

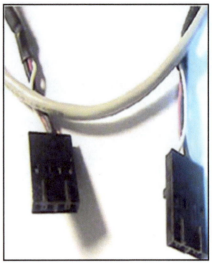

Figure 8: Audio Cable connects CD/DVD drive to the motherboard for sound effect.

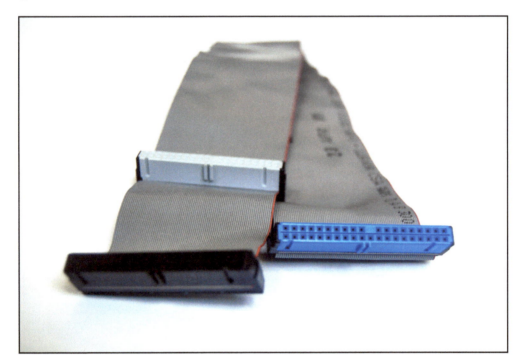

Figure 9: IDE Hard Drive Cable – connects the hard drive and CD/DVD drive to the computer motherboard.

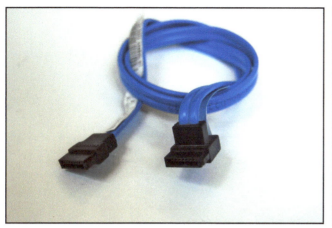

Figure 10: SATA Hard Drive Cable connects hard drive to the motherboard. It is a newer technology. It connects the CD/DVD drive to the motherboard too.

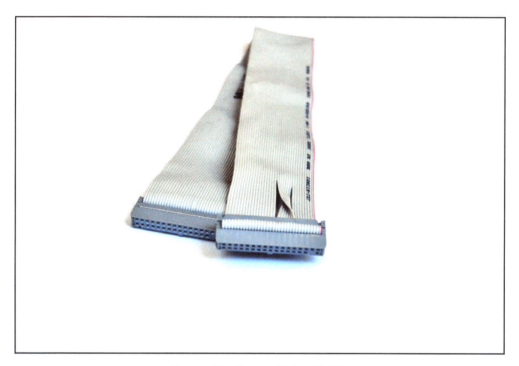

Figure 11: Floppy Drive Cable.

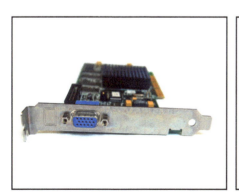

Figure 12A: VGA Adapter.

Figure 12B: VGA Cable

Figure 13A: Firewire Adapter.

Figure 13B: Firewire Cable

SATA Connector (x4)

BIOS Flash Chip
in PLCC Socket

Southbridge
(with heatsink)

Floppy Drive
Connector

IDE Connector (x2)

CMOS Backup Battery

24-pin ATX Power
Connector

Integrated graphics
processor
(with heatsink)

Super IO
Chip

PCI Slot (×3)

DIMM Memory
Slots (×4)

CPU Fan
Connector

CPU Fan &
Heatsink Mount

Integrated audio
codec chip

Integrated Gigabit
Ethernet chip

CPU Socket
(Socket 939)

PCI Express Slot

Connectors For
Integrated Peripherals
PS/2 Keyboard and Mouse, Serial Port,
Parallel Port, VGA, Firewire/IEEE 1394a,
USB (x4), Ethernet, Audio (x6)

Figure 14: How all components connect to the motherboard. (Moxfyre para. 1).

61. Citations

"Adobe Photoshop ® CS4 Extended." Version 11.0 Adobe ™ Systems Inc. ®1990-2008. 5 January 2009.

Challis, Professor Lowrie. Cited in "Warning on wi-fi health risk to children." by Nic Fleming, Medical Correspondent. Telegraph.co.uk 28 Apr 2007. 9 June 2009. <http://www.telegraph.co.uk/news/uknews/1549944/Warning-on-wi-fi-health-risk-to-children.html>

Kozierok, Charles M. "New Technology File System (NTFS)." © 1997-2004. The PC Guide.17 April 2001. 18 May 2009 <http://www.pcguide.com/ref/hdd/file/ntfs/>

Free Software Foundation, Inc.© Hard Drive. "Technology." Wikipedia, The Free Encyclopedia 27 May 2009. <http://en.wikipedia.org/wiki/Hard_disk_drive>

Erin, "Canned Air" WorldStart.com ©2009 4 June, 2009. < http://www.worldstart.com/tips/tips.php/3645>

"Microsoft ® Office Word 2007". (12.0.6425.1000) SP2 MSO. Microsoft Office Enterprise 2007. Microsoft Corporation ®. 2006

"Microsoft ® Outlook 2007" Microsoft Office Enterprise 2007. Microsoft Corporation ®. 2006

Moxfyre, "I created this work entirely by myself." File:Acer E360 Socket 939 motherboard by Foxconn.svg. 13 September, 2008. Foxconn. 25 May 2009 <http://en.wikipedia.org/wiki/File:Acer_E360_Socket_939_motherboard_by_Foxconn.svg>

Munz, Jim. Tech help conversation.. Edgewood College, 3 December, 2008

Sheynkin, Dr Yefim. Online article, "Laptop computers lower sperm counts and increase infertility risk for men. Fertility 11 December 2004. Medical News Today. © 2009. 8 June 2009. <http://www.medicalnewstoday.com/articles/17664.php>

"Spybot - Search & Destroy©®- Overview." Spybot - Search & Destroy.©® 18 May 2009 <http://www.safer-networking.org/en/spybotsd/index.html>

"Windows Vista ™ Home Basic 32BIT". Microsoft Corporation ®. 2007. Dell ™
  Reinstallation DVD 2007. 4 February, 2009.

"Windows XP ™ Professional with Service Pack 3". Microsoft Corporation ® 2007.
  2 February, 2009.

"Windows Update." Microsoft Corporation © 2009. 18 March 2009.
  <http://update.microsoft.com/microsoftupdate/v6/default.aspx?ln=en-
  us&muopt=1>

About the author

Monica Oboagwina, OP is a Systems Engineer at Edgewood College Information Technology Department, Madison, Wisconsin. She has a master's degree in Systematic Theology and is the author of Total Commitment in the Catholic Church, is it Possible? Sister Monica has many published articles, such as "What Mothers Can Do". She is a member of the Dominican Sisters of Sinsinawa.

www.ingramcontent.com/pod-product-compliance
Lightning Source LLC
Chambersburg PA
CBHW041421050326
40689CB00002B/597